TIMELINES

1950s

by
Jane Duden

CRESTWOOD HOUSE

New York

Library of Congress Cataloging In Publication Data
Duden, Jane.
  1950s / by Jane Duden.
  p. cm. — (Timelines)
  Includes index.
  Summary: History, trivia, and fun through photographs and articles present life
in the United States between 1950 and 1959.
  ISBN 0-89686-476-6
  1. United States—History—1945-1953—Juvenile literature. 2. United States—
History—1953-1961—Juvenile literature. 3. History, Modern—1945- —Juvenile
literature. [1. United States—History—1945-1953—Miscellanea. 2. United States—
History—1953-1961—Miscellanea.] I. Title. II. Title: Nineteen fifties. III. Series:
Timelines (New York, N.Y.)
E813.D83   1989   973.921—dc20   89-34400
                                                                            CIP
                                                                            AC

Photo credits
Cover: FPG International: A group of fifties teenagers
Wide World Photos: 4, 7, 8, 9, 11, 12, 13, 14, 15, 16, 20, 22 (right), 24, 25, 26, 27, 29, 32 (left),
    34, 37 (left and right), 38, 41, 42
FPG International: 17, 18, 19, 21, 22 (left), 23, 30, 32 (right), 39, 46; (Jeffry Myers) 45
Ford Motor Company: 35

Macmillan Publishing Company
866 Third Avenue
New York, NY 10022
Collier Macmillan Canada, Inc.

CRESTWOOD HOUSE

Produced by Carnival Enterprises

Printed in the United States of America

First Edition

10 9 8 7 6 5 4 3 2 1

CONTENTS

INTRODUCTION

The 1950s were high-spirited years despite the Korean War. Americans enjoyed new prosperity. After World War II, the United States was more powerful than ever. What Americans wanted most was to build a secure, happy future. First came the baby boom as soldiers returned from war to start families. Then came the housing boom and the development of suburbs, so all those kids could have plenty of fresh air and sunshine. It was a time of family togetherness, favorite TV shows, and Scrabble. The 1950s was also a decade of great fads—Hula-Hoops, Davy Crockett hats, and poodle skirts. It gave us Elvis Presley and rock and roll, crewcuts and sideburns, saddle shoes and white bucks. Even with all this, many Americans felt their way of life was endangered by Soviet Communism. Fearing a nuclear war, many families built fallout shelters in basements and backyards. Many others suffered from poverty and discrimination. So life in the fifties often looked cheerful and comfortable. But real life— with its fears and joys, victories and disappointments—always lurked beneath the surface.

A Korean puppy follows American troops as they march through Korea on the way to the battlefront.

THE GREAT BRINK'S ROBBERY

On January 17, seven armed men dressed in Halloween costumes walked into the Brink's headquarters in Boston. They bound and gagged five employees. Then they emptied the vault of $2.7 million and left. The robbery took less than 20 minutes.

Brink's, Inc. put up a $100,000 reward. Six years passed before the crime was solved. On January 12, 1956, the FBI identified the men behind the holdup. Six were arrested. Two others were already in prison on other charges. One was dead and two were still at large. Unfortunately for Brink's, not a penny of the loot was ever found. What about the reward? That's bad news, too. FBI agents who handled the case had to pass up the money. FBI agents are forbidden to accept such rewards.

WIN A FEW, LOSE A FEW

Census figures said New York led the states in population. Manhattan squeezed 1,938,551 people into its 22 square miles. That made it the most densely populated area in the world. If you wanted more room to roam, you could try Nevada. There you'd have a square mile to yourself! California moved up to number two, the spot Pennsylvania previously held on the population chart.

TUBEGAZING

A survey of TV-watching children 11 to 15 years old revealed shocking news. The story made newspaper headlines in March 1950. Children spent as much time watching TV as they did going to school! Not only that, but homework seemed to take second place to TV for most viewers. People began to worry that good grades would go "down the tube" because of Milton Berle and Ed Sullivan. Could this be the beginning of a new cause for concern?

WORLD WAR III THREATENS

In June 1950, soldiers from Communist North Korea invaded South Korea. The United States was alarmed because South Korea was our ally. President Harry Truman sent troops to help the South Koreans. Communist China, the world's most populous nation, sent troops to help the North Koreans. Russia also sent troops to North Korea. It looked like a third world war would follow.

The war was a big challenge for the United Nations (UN). The UN, only five years old, said the invasion was a violation of world peace. It demanded that Communists leave South Korea. But the Communists kept fighting.

The war ended on July 27, 1953, when the UN and North Korea signed a truce. A permanent peace treaty has never been signed. Korea remains a country divided.

American soldiers prepare for battle in Korea.

The drive-in theater became popular with motorists and, in this theater in Massachusetts, with a pilot.

OUTDOOR MOVIES: THE BIG SCENE!

Americans drove into large, empty fields and hooked their cars up to speakers, and even heaters, to watch movies. The number of drive-in theaters climbed to 2,200. That was twice as many as in 1949! It was enough to drive indoor theater owners to despair. Americans loved their cars, and now drivers could combine their cars with outdoor films. Parents packed up kids in pajamas and headed for the movies. Everyone wondered if drive-in movies were here to stay. Would they put indoor theaters out of business?

HELLO, SNOOPY

Charlie Brown came into the world on October 2. That's the day the *Peanuts* comic strip was first published. Charles M. Schulz created the lovable characters. It was the beginning of a

The first Peanuts *cartoon*

long and happy friendship with kids of all ages, all over the world. It was also the beginning of a multimillion dollar industry. Books, records, sweat shirts, pillows, lunch boxes, and TV specials all brought Charlie and his friends into our homes.

A COLORFUL NEW ERA IN TELEVISION

Color TV. It seemed like a good idea. But would it sell? RCA announced on March 29 that its engineers had developed the first color television for home use. They declared we were on the brink of a new era in television, the era of color. Many viewers wondered what would happen to their black-and-white TV sets. They also wondered if they'd ever be able to afford a color set.

SMOKEY THE BEAR

This was the year a tiny bear cub, singed and scorched, was rescued from a New Mexico forest fire by the United States Forest Service. The little cub was given care and healing and the nickname "Smokey." He went on to live at the National Zoo in Washington. He became the symbol of forest fire safety.

TONS OF TINSEL?

The tallest cut Christmas tree was erected at a shopping center in Seattle, Washington, in December 1950. The Douglas fir stood 221 feet tall. That's about as high as you and 44 friends standing on each other's shoulders!

A MOUNTAIN'S BLAST

An Australian airplane was passing over a peaceful stretch of land in New Guinea. Luckily for the crew and passengers, the pilot was in top form that day, January 21, 1951. Flying over Mount Lamington, he heard what sounded like gunfire. At first, he thought the plane was being shot at. Then the mountain below erupted. It spewed lava and ashes 36,000 feet into the air. The mountain's volcano was believed to be dormant, or inactive. It pounded bits of pumice stone against the aircraft. The pilot guided the plane to safety, away from the erupting volcano. The nearly 3,000 people dwelling near Mount Lamington were not as lucky. They died in the ash clouds that billowed from the volcano's blast.

THE UNDERWATER WORLD CAPTURED

Even as a boy, Jacques-Yves Cousteau had curiosity and a zest for life. He learned to use a simple hand-cranked camera at age 13. He fell in love with the sea during vacations at the Mediterranean shore. He couldn't hold his breath long enough to explore this fascinating underwater world, so with the help of an engineer he invented the Aqualung. That device helps divers breathe underwater. Then in 1951 a diver helped him perfect the first underwater TV camera. Now, thanks to the photographer-inventor's determination and curiosity, we can all marvel at the underwater world of Jacques Cousteau.

THE CRACK HEARD AROUND THE WORLD

It was the ninth inning of the third and final game of the 1951 National League playoffs. The Brooklyn Dodgers were leading 4 to 2. The New York Giants were up to bat with one out. The outlook was gloomy! But Bobby Thomson's bat connected. He walloped a three-run homer! The New York Giants won the game and the 1951 National League pennant.

THE RED SCARE

After the Soviet leader Joseph Stalin broke peace agreements with Europe and the United States, Americans grew fearful about the spread of Communism. So when Julius and Ethel Rosenberg were convicted in March of stealing atomic bomb secrets and giving them to the Soviet Union, it became one of the biggest news stories of the 1950s. The Rosenbergs, parents of two young sons, said they were innocent. But they were called spies and sentenced to death. For two years, they fought to get the courts to change the verdict. On June 19, 1953, the Rosenbergs were executed in the electric chair. It was the first time in American history that a husband and wife were put to death for a crime. More than 5,000 people gathered in New York to protest the executions.

Julius and Ethel Rosenberg arrive at the federal courthouse in New York.

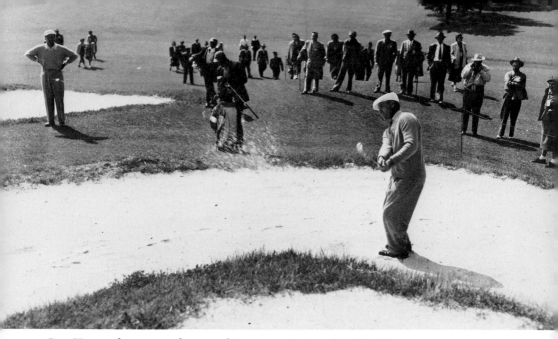

Ben Hogan clears a sand trap on his way to winning the 1951 Masters Tournament.

THE MASTERS JACKET

Golfer Ben Hogan and his wife Valerie were on their way home to Texas after being in a golf tournament in Arizona. He saw a huge bus go into a skid. Ben knew they were about to be hit. As the crushing collision came, Ben threw his body across his wife's to protect her. That move saved them both. Valerie had only slight injuries. But Ben was in bad shape. Only his groans alerted rescuers that he was alive. Doctors performed many operations on Ben. He spent 58 days in a hospital bed. Doctors told Ben he might walk again, but certainly would never golf again. Ben Hogan refused to accept that news. With the spirit that had earned him the name "Bantam Ben," he fought back. Within a year he was playing golf again. Two years later, in 1951, Ben Hogan won the Masters Tournament in Augusta, Georgia. Ben Hogan had earned the grandest title and prize a golfer could get. He wore the Masters "green jacket" with pride.

TRY, TRY AGAIN

A scared William Howard Mays stepped up to the plate on May 25, 1951. He wanted to show the crowd in Philadelphia that he could bat major-league style. But as 21,820 fans in the stadium watched, poor Willie struck out. That would not be the only failure that haunted Willie Mays. The next 26 times he got up to bat, Mays made only one hit. Just as the baseball world began to write him off, Willie started to hit and run with a fury. He was named Rookie of the Year in 1951. He was named Player of the Year in 1954. Today he is known as one of baseball's greats.

Willie Mays

WALK, DON'T RUN

New York City put up its first four "Don't Walk" signs in busy Times Square on February 29, 1952. "Walk" flashed for 22 seconds. "Don't Walk" flashed for 58 seconds. Walkers had to move quickly! Two months before, New York had switched to its first three-color traffic lights—red, amber, green—in an attempt to reduce accidents.

A CRAZY DREAM . . . OR IS IT?

Wernher von Braun started dreaming about space flight when he was 18. He brought his dreams with him when he came from Germany to live in the United States in 1945. On May 15, 1952, he suggested that scientists start building a space vehicle that could take pilots to Mars! You can bet that "way out" idea made headlines and got laughs. But space experts eventually learned to pay attention when Wernher von Braun had an idea. His dreams had a tendency to come true. He helped design and build the first space rocket.

Many scientists, astronauts, and politicians now believe humans might head to Mars by the year 2010. The mission would take off from an orbiting space station. The trip to Mars would take two to three years.

New traffic lights attempt to control traffic in New York City.

Dick Clark on the set of "American Bandstand"

ROCK 'N' ROLL TV

"American Bandstand" was the first national TV show devoted exclusively to rock and roll. Kids formed fan clubs. They sent more than 50,000 letters a week to Dick Clark. From Maine to California, teens gathered around TV sets to watch top rock stars perform their latest hits. They thought watching the "Spotlight Dance" on "American Bandstand" was more important than homework. Some kids did more than watch. They lined up outside the studio to get into the television dance party. They rocked and rolled before the cameras. The Doors, Linda Ronstadt, Simon and Garfunkel, the Supremes, the Temptations, and Stevie Wonder all got started on "American Bandstand." The teens judged the new songs themselves. "It's easy to dance to. I'll give it a ten," became the highest form of praise.

COOL IDEA!

General Motors announced on July 14 it had perfected an air-conditioning unit for automobiles. It was offered as an option on some of GM's 1953 cars.

Hank Aaron, Home Run King

THE HOMER THAT DIDN'T COUNT

Eventually, Hank Aaron would become the "Home Run King," retiring with 40 more home runs than the great Babe Ruth. But no one predicted such fame for Hank on the day he hit his first home run as a pro. Hank got so excited that he missed first base. When the opposing team complained, Hank Aaron was called out. What did he learn from the blunder? Sportswriters say he never again watched the ball's flight but set his sights on touching first base.

A STRANGE CAREER IS OVER

Alvin "Shipwreck" Kelly had an odd career. When he was a sailor, he survived dozens of shipwrecks at sea. But here's how he got his fame: As a professional stuntman in the 1920s, he perched atop flagpoles. In Atlantic City he once stayed on top of a flagpole for 49 days. "I just went up for a breath of fresh air," he explained.

Movie fans enjoy the new craze of 1952—3-D glasses.

Shipwreck Kelly started a fad with his flagpole sitting. But it was a career that didn't last. In October 1952, the once-famous flagpole sitter was found dead from a heart attack in the streets of New York. He was penniless. Stuffed in his pockets were faded newspaper clippings of his days of fame and glory.

A FAD THAT FIZZLED

The movie industry needed a boost. Its audience had been cut in half by tough competition—television. It needed a gimmick to get folks back in the theaters. In 1952, the industry thought it had found one.

"Man-eating lions and beasts that leap right out of the screen!" was the way one ad lured moviegoers to the first 3-D movie in November 1952. (3-D stands for three-dimensional.) People put on cardboard 3-D glasses to view *Bwana Devil*. Lions leapt into their laps. Trains roared down on them. Arrows shot into their theater! People loved the optical illusions created by the 3-D glasses. But the fad didn't last long.

Tenley Albright, left, consoles a young skater who broke her wrist during a figure-skating championship.

VICTORY OVER POLIO

When Tenley Albright won the world figure-skating championship, it was a double victory. She was the first American to win the world honor. She was also the first winner who had overcome the dread disease of polio to do it. A 17-year-old ice ballerina from Boston who had been skating since age nine, Albright received the unanimous vote of the judges. The victory capped her six-year comeback from polio. She was runner-up in the 1952 Olympics.

18   *Jim Thorpe, right, was the first Native American to win fame on the football field.*

ALL-AMERICAN RAVES

The song everybody was singing was "Doggie in the Window." The TV show everybody was watching was "Ozzie and Harriet." The couple everybody was admiring was Senator John Kennedy and his bride, Jacqueline. And the truce that everybody was cheering was the one that stopped the war in Korea.

TOWN HONORS SPORTS HERO

When Jim Thorpe died in 1953, he was considered one of America's greatest athletes. He played professional football during the first half of the 20th century. He was the first Native American to have done so. Thorpe was a Sac and Fox Indian, from two tribes originating in Pennsylvania. A year after he died, a town was created in his honor. The three small communities of Lower, Upper and East Mauch Chunk, Pennsylvania, joined together and became Jim Thorpe, Pennsylvania. It had a population of 5,300.

Edmund Hillary (left) and Tenzing Norgay (right), the first men to reach the top of Mount Everest, with John Hunt, another member of the climbing expedition

FASTER THAN SOUND

On May 18, 1953, Jacqueline Cochran became the first woman to break the sound barrier. She flew faster than the speed of sound. One of America's top pilots, Cochran sent sonic booms over the California desert several times. She pulled out of steep dives at speeds of over 760 miles per hour. Cochran was a Lieutenant Colonel in the United States Air Force Reserve. And on May 18 she was a smiling daredevil!

"HI" FROM THE TOP OF THE WORLD!

Many climbers had tried to scale Mount Everest, the highest mountain in the world. It wasn't until May 29, 1953, that two men finally made it. Sir Edmund Hillary of New Zealand and his Nepalese Sherpa guide, Tenzing Norgay, were the first climbers to reach the top.

New York Yankees manager Casey Stengel

They had to overcome a number of challenges to do it. The mountain is in the Himalaya Mountain Range, between the countries of Tibet and Nepal in Asia. Avalanches, crevasses, strong winds, and steep rises make climbing Everest especially dangerous. A few climbers are also scared off by stories of a creature called the Abominable Snowman. Sherpa tribespeople believe it lives around Mount Everest. But climbers still keep coming for that mighty challenge of climbing to the top of the world.

NEVER BEFORE IN BASEBALL

The celebration was incredible! But so was the reason for celebrating. The Yankees had won their fifth straight World Series, a feat never before achieved. Casey Stengel became the first manager to match five straight pennants with five successive world titles. He did it in his first five years in the American League.

MAKE A BIRTHDAY WISH!

How many times have you had a birthday wish come true? It pays to keep trying, because sometimes wishes do come true. On January 4, 1954, an unknown singer celebrated his 19th birthday. He brought his guitar to a Memphis studio and paid $4.00 to record two songs. His name? Elvis Presley.

THE FOUR-MINUTE MILE AT LAST!

For 20 years, human runners had been trying to run a mile in less than four minutes. Could anyone ever run a mile faster? On May 6, 1954, British athlete Roger Bannister did it! He ran a mile in three minutes, 59.4 seconds. Bannister's record was broken a month later by John Landy, an Australian runner.

A BATTLE BEGINS

Linda Brown was a young black schoolgirl living in Topeka, Kansas, in the 1950s. She traveled more than two miles to a black elementary school. Just four blocks from her home was a white school. Her parents sued the school district for its policy of school segregation. The lawsuit turned into one of the most far-reaching cases of this century. On May 17, 1954, the United States Supreme Court ordered schools to open their classrooms to all children. Linda Brown played an important part in that change in American education.

Bill Haley (seated) and the Comets

In 1954, 8.5 million white children and 2.5 million black children went to segregated schools in the southern states. They were greatly affected by the new law.

ONE O'CLOCK, TWO O'CLOCK, THREE O'CLOCK ROCK

The "Nation's Rockingest Rhythm Group" in 1954 was Bill Haley and the Comets. Their song, "Crazy, Man, Crazy" hit number 14 on the Billboard charts. Their new song, "(We're Gonna) Rock Around the Clock," was another up and coming hit.

Left: Many blacks fought for the right to go to the same schools as whites.
Right: Roger Bannister breaks the four-minute mile.

CRUTCHES, CANES . . . AND THE CURE

Can you imagine dreading summer? When polio became an epidemic in the 1950s summer became a scary time. That was the season when polio struck children, almost always leaving them crippled in some way. Worried parents warned children to stay away from mud puddles and swimming pools. These were suspected breeding spots for the virus. Kids were warned not to drink out of the same glass others used. They could not get too tired. They had to be sure to tell a parent if they got headaches. Many children died from polio. Those who survived often had to learn how to walk again, wearing leg braces or using crutches. Some children had to stay in iron lungs. The iron lung was a huge machine that helped a patient breathe.

Then in 1953 Dr. Jonas Salk developed a vaccine to guard against polio. In February 1954, the polio vaccine was first given to schoolchildren in Pittsburgh. Soon after, the vaccine was given to every school-age child in America. Today, thanks to Dr. Salk's vaccine, parents and kids no longer have to dread summer and the feared disease polio.

A polio patient receives treatment in an iron lung.

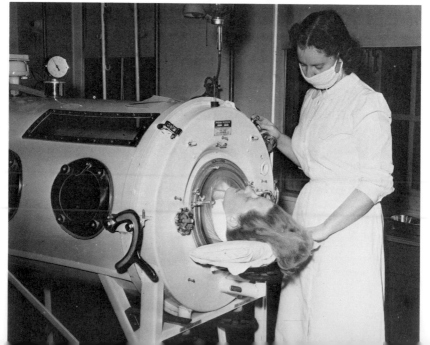

Fess Parker played Davy Crockett in the 1950s.

KING OF THE WILD FRONTIER

Walt Disney had another winner. In 1954, he turned a western hero named Davy Crockett into a TV series and then a movie. Davy's coonskin cap became a trademark, and caps began selling like hotcakes. For seven months, an admiring public spent millions of dollars on the hats. They also bought Davy Crockett swimsuits, toy guns and knives, bows and arrows, leggings and moccasins, pajamas and bedspreads, lunch boxes and guitars. "The Ballad of Davy Crockett" was recorded in 16 versions. But before the year was over, children lost interest. Davy Crockett souvenir-buying faded away as quickly as it had begun.

SLOW LEARNER OR GENIUS?

If your child didn't speak until age three or talk much until age nine, would you worry? Albert Einstein's parents did. They worried about his shyness and his inability to learn. They surely didn't think he'd someday be one of the world's foremost geniuses—the father of modern math and science.

Albert Einstein died on April 8, 1955. Many people thought the answer to his genius might be found in his brain. Scientists removed his brain for study and tests. But they found nothing unusual about it.

"SHOE"

On May 7, 1955, jockey Willie ("Shoe") Shoemaker won his first Kentucky Derby. When he was born, no one guessed he'd win more than 9,000 races in his lifetime. He weighed only two-and-a-half pounds at birth and was small enough to fit into a shoebox. The doctor said he was so tiny and cold that he wouldn't live through the night. But Willie Shoemaker's grandma didn't give up. Far from a hospital and modern infant care, she laid him on pillows on the stove door. The heat from the oven kept him warm.

Willie didn't let his small size keep him from sports or horses. And he didn't let his age keep him from winning. He won his fourth Kentucky Derby when he was 54 years old.

Willie Shoemaker (Number 7) takes his horse Swap to the finish line in the 1955 Kentucky Derby.

Mac and Dick McDonald's first hamburger stand

MILKSHAKES TO MILLIONS

The McDonald boys, Mac and Dick, spent a lot of time in their California hamburger place. They turned out french fries and fifteen-cent hamburgers in a flash. This was the first fast food restaurant. Ray Kroc, a milkshake machine salesman, saw the boys keeping his machines busy. He pictured an assembly line idea for turning out hot-off-the-grill, take-them-with-you burgers at low price. Busy Americans in a hurry would surely go for that idea! The brothers agreed to sell Ray Kroc the rights to their fast food restaurant and in 1955 Kroc started his first McDonald's in Chicago. Ray built an empire of drive-in restaurants with golden arches and "McDonald's" spelled out in big letters. The rest is history.

STRANGE CREATURES AND SAUCERLIKE THINGS

The way Billy Ray Taylor told it, August 21, 1955, had been a hot night on the Sutton farm in Kentucky. He had gone outside to get a drink from the well. As he drank, he saw a large, bright object come out of the sky. It landed about 300 feet away from him. It was silver and shot out colored flames. Billy ran to tell his friends and family inside about it, but they didn't believe him.

An hour later, at 8 P.M., they, too, looked out to see aliens coming toward the farmhouse. The creatures were four feet tall and had long skinny arms and large heads. A yellow glow surrounded them. Frightened, two of the farmers picked up shotguns and fired at the creatures. The creatures simply somersaulted and disappeared into the night. Later, they came back, peeking into windows, sitting on the roof, and perching in trees. Again, the men went out with guns. The shooting lasted for hours.

When the creatures vanished, Taylor and his friends took off for the police station in town. They all reported the amazing incident. The police followed them back to check it out. Just as they got back to the farm, some meteors streaked out of the sky with a loud swishing sound. Even though bullet holes were everywhere, the police would not believe the Sutton farm story. The U.S. Air Force could not confirm any sightings. But the eight adults and three children who were at that farmhouse knew they had seen strange creatures who squinted and did not like the lights inside the house. It had not been the bullets that kept them away, they believed . . . it was the lights.

SITTING DOWN FOR HER RIGHTS

Mrs. Rosa Parks, a middle-aged black seamstress, was tired as she boarded the bus in downtown Montgomery, Alabama, on December 1. Carrying heavy groceries, she paid the dime fare

Before the civil rights movement, blacks were allowed to sit only in the last seats on buses.

and sat in the first seat she came upon. It was a seat that by law was reserved for "whites only." The bus driver ordered Mrs. Parks to give up her seat for white passengers. But Mrs. Parks refused to move. She was just too tired. Her feet hurt and her groceries were heavy. A police officer was called. Mrs. Parks was arrested.

The news of Mrs. Parks's arrest stirred up anger among black Americans in Montgomery. A black minister named Martin Luther King, Jr., urged all blacks to boycott Montgomery's city buses. The boycott was a nonviolent way for blacks to protest the unfairness of the law. By sitting down on the bus that day, Rosa Parks stood up for what she believed in. She started the Montgomery bus boycott. It became the opening act of the civil rights movement.

1956

NAME THAT TUNE AND WIN BIG BUCKS!

Is winning a lot of money one of your dreams? Fourteen-year-old George Wright III had that dream come true. George was on the TV quiz show "The Big Surprise" on February 4, 1956, and he got the surprise. He identified the title and sang the chorus of a 1920s song hit, "Me and My Shadow." George won $100,000. He had between $30,000 and $50,000 left after taxes were paid on the winnings. That left plenty for his wish of buying a tipple—a sort of ukulele. The rest went into a fund for college.

BLACKS RIDE WITH EQUAL RIGHTS

The Supreme Court ruled in April that bus companies in the South could no longer force blacks to sit at the back of the bus. Segregation in public transportation was ruled unconstitutional. The "whites only" signs came down from the fronts of buses. It was a happy day, but the tension wasn't over. The bus boycott, organized by Dr. Martin Luther King, continued until

Martin Luther King, Jr.

black bus drivers were hired for mainly black bus routes. The struggle for equal rights still had many more battles to win.

BIRD DIAPERS

That's right. Bertha Dlugi wanted her bird to fly freely around her house. But she didn't want the mess that might come with it. So she invented a bird diaper. In 1956, she received a patent on her invention.

GREAT CONNECTIONS

Freeways changed the face of America, starting in 1956. That's the year our great interstate highway system was begun. President Eisenhower signed the bill in June. He okayed billions of dollars to build a nationwide network of highways. Americans were traveling more often and for longer distances. Trucks were replacing railroads for shipping food and many products. Drivers wanted direct routes without traffic lights. Planners proposed a network of highways that would connect America's major cities. Today we travel coast to coast with the same interstate road system that was begun in 1956—and it's still growing!

AMERICANS LIKE IKE

Dwight D. Eisenhower was re-elected president in the 1956 election. It was the greatest landslide since Franklin D. Roosevelt swamped Alfred M. Landon in 1936. Perhaps TV coverage helped. The former WWII general and "the man with the big grin" was the first president to have a television news conference. It aired on January 19, 1955. On June 6, 1955, he became the first to have a telecast in color. His October birthdate might have helped him win the election, too. More presidents have been born in October than in any other month.

SHAKE, RATTLE ... AND HERE COMES ROCK AND ROLL!

He was known as "Elvis the Pelvis" because he bumped and rolled his hips to the beat of his electric guitar. This 21-year-old Memphis truck driver sang, shouted, and crooned. Teenage girls screamed and fainted when Elvis Presley moved closer to the audience. Parents didn't allow their teenagers to watch him perform or listen to his music. Boyfriends threatened to break up with their girlfriends if they went to his performances. Girls who went to his performances came home and broke up with their guys.

Elvis Presley introduced us to rock and roll—but many did not think it was here to stay. His music was an amazing blend of country, rock, blues, and gospel. Adults protested, "His music will corrupt our children. You can't even dance to it. It'll never last!" Ed Sullivan, host of a weekly TV variety show, called Elvis "unfit for a family audience."

Young people didn't agree. They mobbed Elvis's concerts. They bought millions of his records. In 1956, "Don't Be Cruel" and "You Ain't Nothing But a Hound Dog" became the longest-lasting number one rock and roll singles in music history. Both were number one for eleven weeks. When Ed Sullivan changed his mind, Elvis appeared on his September 9 show. Still, Elvis could only be shown from the waist up, so as not to shock the viewers.

A SMALL MAN MAKES IT BIG

Fifteen-year-old Edson Arantes do Nascimento's mom scolded him when he snuck a soccer ball into bed with him at night. She didn't want her son playing soccer. They were a poor family. Her son had little chance of being noticed. But he kept practicing with his neighborhood friends. His friends nicknamed him "Pelé." Edson did not really like the name, but it stuck.

Despite his mother's doubts, Pelé was discovered. In 1956 Pelé scored so many goals that the national team of his country, Brazil, found a spot for him! Fans were shocked and pleased that this small "giant" would play all the way to the World Games.

Pelé came to America years later in 1975 when the New York Cosmos signed him. Fans in the United States were crazy about Pelé. They were glad his mother's predictions had proved wrong!

PERFECT!

It was the World Series's only no-hit game. In fact, it was perfect — meaning no Dodger ever made it to first base. Don Larsen of the New York Yankees made baseball history in 1956. He pitched the game against the Brooklyn Dodgers in the 1956 World Series. His pitches helped the New York Yankees win their 17th pennant. That game was a once-in-a-lifetime moment in sports.

NO MORE SHOTS!

Thank Dr. Albert Sabin if you'd rather swallow your polio vaccine than get it through a needle. On October 6, Dr. Sabin announced a new polio vaccine that could be taken by mouth. It first had to be tested for safety on humans. Large-scale tests started with prison volunteers in 1957. When the vaccine proved safe, the oral vaccine replaced the Salk shot.

Left: Elvis Presley   Right: Pelé (right)

TOPS IN TENNIS

Althea Gibson was so poor that she could not afford a tennis racquet or lessons. Worse, even if she could, she would not have been allowed to play in most tennis tournaments because she was black. But a playground leader was impressed by the way Althea played paddle tennis in a park near her home in New York City. He bought her a tennis racquet, and Althea became a winner.

Althea was so good she attracted the attention of Alice Marble, a famous white tennis player. Alice had won the tennis "superbowl"—Wimbledon. Fans admired and listened to her. Alice said Althea should be allowed to play anyone, white or black.

Soon after, Althea became the first black person invited to enter the National Championship tournament in Forest Hills, New York. Seven years later, on July 6, 1957, Althea Gibson stood in the center court of the world tournament at England's Wimbledon. The Queen of England and 16,000 fans watched as Althea won the match in less than an hour. "At last, at last," Althea whispered to herself. She waved to her roaring fans.

Ford's Edsel

DETROIT'S FIRST BIG FLOP

In August, Ford's first new line of cars in over a decade rolled off the Detroit assembly lines. The car was the Edsel, named after the only son of Henry Ford. Three years of research and planning went into the Edsel. Millions of dollars had been spent in preparations to make the car. It was to be the American family's dream car. Advertising events for the Edsel built suspense.

When the Edsel was finally unveiled, curious shoppers flocked to car showrooms. But few came to buy. Ford did everything it could to get the Edsels on the road. It offered bonuses and cut prices. People wouldn't buy them. They wouldn't even steal them. During the time Edsels were being manufactured, only one Edsel was reported stolen.

By November 1959, Ford called it quits and stopped making Edsels. The company lost millions of dollars. The Edsel was the auto industry's first major flop. What went wrong? Experts sum it up by saying it was the wrong car for the wrong market at the wrong time.

Edsel owners who kept the cars have been able to sell them to classic car buyers for big profits. And the English language got a new slang word for error and failure—"Edsel."

Althea Gibson in Wimbledon's quarterfinals

35

IS TV IN TROUBLE?

ABC, CBS, and NBC had more open time spots than they could sell for the new fall TV season. It looked like television's first unprofitable season in its ten-year history. Could the slump be due to boring TV shows? One new idea was pay TV. Viewers could see good things on pay TV and medium or poor shows on free television. In 1957, networks decided to stick to the tried-and-true formula—westerns and situation comedies. Some of the popular shows were "Father Knows Best" and "Roy Rogers."

LAIKA, ANIMALNAUT

The first animal to go into space orbit was a female Samoyed named Laika. In November 1957, she was sent into orbit by the Soviets. She would orbit Earth in one of their first satellites. They wanted to see the effects of space travel on a living creature, without risking a human life. Unfortunately, they did not yet know how to bring Laika and the satellite back home. Laika died when the capsule ran out of oxygen. It set off a worldwide outcry from animal lovers.

Three years later, in August 1960, the Soviet Union sent two more dogs, Stelka and Belka, into space. This time the flight lasted just 24 hours. The capsule parachuted safely to Earth. The animals were reported to be fine. Luckily, many changes in the space program have been made since those days. The safety of humans and animals now receives careful planning and attention.

THE CAT IN THE HAT AND ALL OF THAT

Theodor Geisel, also known as Dr. Seuss, wrote a fun book. But no publishers liked it. "Who on earth wants to read about a cat in a hat? The pictures are odd and the rhymes are even worse," said the publishers.

36

But Dr. Seuss didn't give up. In 1957, Random House saw things differently and published *The Cat in the Hat*. The book caught on with adults who had a hard time giving up their copies to their kids.

CLEAN-CUT CROONER

Just when the rock and roll craze had many parents in a panic, Pat Boone saved the day. The clean-cut singer had smooth manners, a gleaming smile, and white buckskin shoes. He was a top Ivy League student and later the father of four daughters. He had three million-selling records: "I'll Be Home," "I Almost Lost My Mind," and "Ain't That a Shame." Much of his music jumped with a rock and roll dance beat. The difference was that Pat, unlike Elvis, stood still when he sang. A huge new audience approved and looked for more!

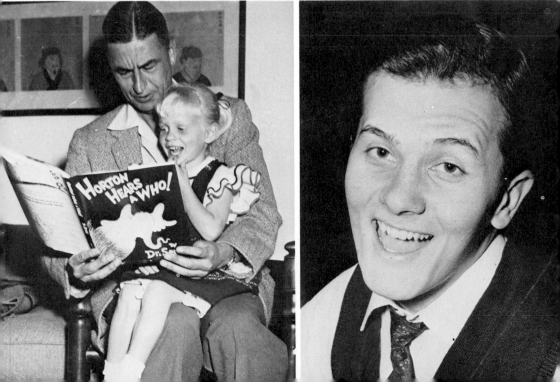

Left: Theodor Geisel reads to a young fan. Right: Twenty-two-year-old Pat Boone

HOW'S YOUR CHESS GAME?

If you want to learn chess, there's no time like the present. Just think of Bobby Fischer's example. Bobby's older sister taught him to play chess when he was six. In 1958, when he was 15, he earned the title of International Grand Master. He was the youngest person in the world to win that title!

A GUITAR FOR A GUN

Elvis Presley traded in his rock and roll crown for an army uniform on March 24. The 23-year-old singing star had sold over 40 million records in two years. He didn't seem to mind that his earnings would fall from more than $100,000 to just $83.20 a month. Elvis said, "I'm looking forward to serving in

International Grand Master Bobby Fischer

Elvis Presley answers questions about entering the army.

the army. I think it will be a great experience for me." Hordes of brokenhearted fans were more worried about the two years he'd be away in the service than Elvis was.

HULA-HOOPS MAKE HOOPLA

Who ever would have guessed that a length of plastic molded into a ring would earn millions of dollars for two toymakers? The toy manufacturer, Wham-O, began selling the plastic rings for $1.98. They called them Hula-Hoops. Within a few months, American kids were spinning 30 million hoops. They spun the hoops in houses, playgrounds, schools, and backyards across the nation! The fad turned into a frenzy.

The instructions said "Hug the hoop to the backside. Push hard with the right hand . . . now rock . . . swing it . . . sway it . . .

you got it." Toymakers said the Hula-Hoop was bigger than the Davy Crockett fad or anything else in the toy business. You could Hula-Hoop it alone, or get into a giant-size hoop with a partner. One Hula-Hooper made news swinging 14 different hoops at a time. It was a great stunt, good exercise, and fun for contests. Hula-Hoops were the biggest fad to hit the United States since the yo-yo.

"HIT IT!"

On August 17, 1958, Harry Cordello yelled words that would change his life forever. Harry was blind and had a heart murmur. His parents worried about his playing games with other children. Harry became lonely and spent most of his time listening to TV and daydreaming.

As he grew older, doctors found that Harry's heart murmur had disappeared. They urged him to try more physical exercise. That's when one of his teachers helped Harry take a "risk." The teacher got Harry to a lake, put him into a life jacket and water skis, and handed him a tow rope. Not knowing what to expect, Harry somehow worked up the courage to yell, "Hit it!" Those words did more than signal the boat driver to take off. They changed Harry's life.

After Harry learned to ski, he spent a lot of time swimming. He even swam across San Francisco Bay despite its heavy currents and undertows. Later Harry's favorite sport became long-distance running. He ran more than 50 marathons with a sighted person as his guide.

Harry started life as a blind and sickly child. He turned into a champ. Next time you face a tough challenge or new risk, think of Harry's words: "You must never be afraid to try, and you must never be afraid of failing. To fail is not the worst thing in the world. After you have failed ten times, you will appreciate all the more success that comes with the eleventh try."

Harry Winston shows off the Hope diamond before donating it to the Smithsonian Institution in Washington.

NOT MUCH HOPE FOR OWNERS

There was once a 112-carat steel-blue diamond embedded in a statue of a Hindu god. In 1642, a thief stole it. Bad luck followed: He was mauled to death by wild dogs. Marie Antoinette owned the jewel in the late 1700s but did not wear it to her death at the chopping block. A British banking family named Hope owned the gem in the 1800s, but they went broke. Around 1900, a Turkish sultan's lady wore the diamond before her untimely death. A former owner of the *Washington Post* newspaper had it before his son died in a car crash and his daughter killed herself. The man died as a patient in a mental asylum. On November 8, 1958, the $1.5 million Hope diamond was given to the Smithsonian Institution. The owner, jeweler Harry Winston, probably felt relief!

Thirty-five students at Southeast Missouri State College joined in the latest fad and stuffed themselves into a campus phone booth.

SOMEBODY ANSWER THAT PHONE

Have you ever felt crowded in a telephone booth? Imagine 18 other bodies stuffed in there with you! Crowding into telephone booths was a big fad in 1959. Most of the stuffing took place in California, usually by guys unafraid of bruises. One phone booth at the University of California, Los Angeles, held 17 people. Eighteen students stuffed themselves into a phone booth at the College of St. Mary's in Moraga, California. But 34 students fit into a booth at Modesto Junior College. The trick to that was tipping the phone booth over onto the ground. "No fair!" yelled

42

many. They opened up a debate on the correct way to stuff a phone booth. It didn't matter much, though. The fad ended the same year it began.

ALASKA BECOMES 49TH STATE

When Alaska joined the Union on January 3, 1959, it was the first new state in almost 47 years. People laughed at Secretary of State William H. Seward when he bought Alaska from Russia in 1867 for two cents an acre. They thought it was a foolish waste of money to buy a wilderness of ice and snow. They nicknamed it Seward's Folly and Seward's Icebox. But not for long! Alaska turned out to be rich in fish, minerals, timber, and other resources. The value of these resources has paid back the purchase price hundreds of times over.

NOW HIRING ASTRONAUTS

How do you think the job description for an astronaut would sound? Must have patience, courage, strength, and not be afraid of heights? In 1959, the Mercury Project was created. It was the first United States space program that would launch Americans into space. The National Aeronautics and Space Administration (NASA) needed people to apply for the job. Ever since the Soviet Union had launched its Sputnik in 1957, the United States had been behind in the space race. Now was the time to get serious.

In early 1959, 110 test pilots were chosen to go through a rigorous screening. Applying to be an astronaut was tough. It meant weeks of hard mental and physical stress tests. The list of candidates was slowly cut from 110 to 69 to 32 to 18. In April, seven men were chosen. One of the pilots, John Glenn, became a popular spokesperson for the group. With his boyish grin, he declared that being one of the first men in space "probably would be the nearest to heaven I will ever get."

43

YOU'VE COME A LONG WAY, BARBIE

At first, she was a fad. Now she's a tradition. Barbie was introduced by Mattel, Inc. on March 1, 1959. By the time she turned 25, over 200 million Barbie dolls and other members of her family had been sold worldwide.

It started when Ruth Handler thought her daughter would like a doll to dress in miniature fashions instead of dressing up paper dolls. So Ruth and Elliot Handler, the brains and money behind Mattel, Inc., created the Barbie doll. She was named after the Handlers' pre-teen daughter, Barbie.

The original brunette Barbie created in 1959 sells for more than $700 today.

A BIG FISH STORY

Have you ever wondered what the biggest fish ever caught was? It was a 2,664-pound white shark pulled in by Alfred Dean off Ceduna, Australia, on April 21, 1959.

OUR "LAST WILDERNESS"

It's the windiest, the coldest, the quietest, the loneliest continent. Except for a few mountain peaks and rocks, 98 percent of Antarctica is covered by a cap of ice and snow up to three miles thick. Some people felt the world's fifth-largest continent would be a great place for military maneuvers, forts or bases, and weapons testing. They wanted to dump radioactive waste and trash there. Others disagreed. They were scientists discovering a wealth of clues about wildlife, weather, and centuries past. They were learning about the role Antarctica plays in determining our climate.

The question of how to use Antarctica was settled in 1959. Twelve nations signed the Antarctic Treaty. Many scientists now live and study there. The scientific research is a chance for nations to share their findings and join together in friendship. Who knows what will be learned to help humanity, thanks to the Antarctic Treaty?

A MOST VALUABLE SPORTSMAN

Most sports have a Most Valuable Player Award (MVP) at the end of their All-Star games. It is highly prized. In 1959, there was an unexpected tie at the end of the Pro-Basketball All-Star game. Veteran Bob Pettit and rookie Elgin Baylor were the winners. Still, there was only one trophy to be awarded. True sportsmanship takes place both on and off the court, as demonstrated by Bob Pettit. As he shook Elgin Baylor's hand, he told him, "You take it. I've won the award before. I can wait for my duplicate." Rookie Elgin Baylor was grateful to be able to walk off the court with an award in his hands from his first professional season.

CARS, CARS, CARS

By 1959, the average car cost $1,180. Cars also began to cost a lot in terms of American lives. For the first time in history, the total number of deaths from car accidents surpassed the total number of American deaths in wars.

By the end of the 1950s, Americans had become a car culture. People went everywhere and did almost everything in their cars.

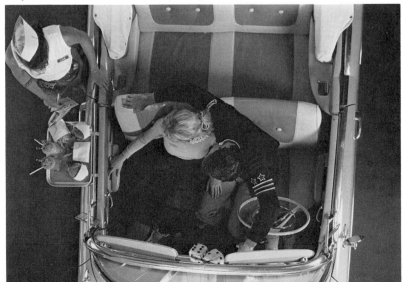

Elvis Presley rocks to his hit song, "You Ain't Nothing But a Hound Dog."

INDEX